Money

Contents

Teachers' notes	1	Count up to £1	20
Games with coin cards	5	Count-ups	22
Coin cards	6	More count-ups	23
More coin cards	8	£5 notes	24
Jumble Sale matching cards	10	£10 notes	25
Make your own Jumble Sale matching cards	12	Teddy shop A	26
Jumble story	13	Teddy shop B	27
The ten pence game	14	Flap puzzles 1 and 2	28
'The ten pence game' playing cards	15	Flap puzzles 3 and 4	29
The fifty pence game	16	Make your own flap puzzles	30
'The fifty pence game' playing cards	17	Bus fares	31
Count up to 50p	18	Jumble toys	32

Teachers' notes

Aim of this book
The aim of this book is to provide you with well-presented and mathematically valuable supplementary material which will link with your existing scheme of work for mathematics, and which children will also enjoy using. To help you make the best use of the activities, please read the notes which follow.

Printing
Although photocopying on to white paper may be the simplest way for you to copy the activities in this book, do consider other alternatives. Some pages benefit from copying directly on to card, while others look much more interesting when printed on coloured paper or card. If your school does not have the facilities to do this, you may be able to have copies made using a duplicator or printing machine at a larger primary school or secondary school close to you, or perhaps at a teachers' centre.

To keep re-usable cards or worksheets in good condition, put them inside plastic wallets, laminate them, or cover them with clear sticky plastic. Even copies made on paper are surprisingly strong when covered.

Record-keeping and storage
We have not provided a separate system of record-keeping for these activities, as most teachers prefer to add to their existing scheme of records. You could use the child's own maths writing book to make a note of activities used, when this would be helpful information to have. Worksheets can usually be fastened into the child's book using a piece of sticky tape at the side, like an extra page in the book, as an obvious reminder of an activity completed.

Mathematical content
This book provides activities to help children with recognising coins and notes, exchanging them for others and counting up amounts of money. Some activities require the children to compare amounts of money, to pay with exactly the right amount of money or to give change. Amounts of money are shown as coins, and by using figures or words. Written work is linked to practical activity, and the children are given the opportunity to make up questions and problems for each other. Coins, notes and calculators may be used to solve or check a problem.

Every activity needs introducing by the teacher if the children are to make the most of it. Sometimes, activities may be taken home to talk about with parents or other family members.

Although this book concentrates predominantly on problems using either pence or pounds, you will find that as the children grow in confidence they can extend many of the activities to use pounds and pence together.

◆ ESSENTIALS FOR MATHS: Money

Notes on individual activities

Pages 5–9: Games with coin cards

These hexagonal playing cards give children practice in seeing that you can represent the same amount of money in many ways using coins. The cards use amounts up to twenty pence only.

Print these pages on to card. Use different colours if you want to make more than one set, to make it easier to sort them out. Cover the pages in clear sticky plastic before cutting them out, to give the cards a longer life. Store them in an A4 wallet or zip-top bag.

Before using the suggestions on page 5, some children benefit from an introductory session where they just choose a card, put the right coins on top of the coin pictures, and then count up the total. This also gives you an opportunity to check that the children are familiar with the names of the coins and the fact that, for example, you can exchange five one-pence coins for a five pence piece.

Pages 10–13: 'Jumble sale' activities

Print pages 10 and 11 on to card, colour them in if you wish, and cut them up to make a set of 15 matching cards and a title card. The cards show amounts from ten pence to fifty pence represented with coins, prices using figures and the price in words.

This is a good activity for a child to do with an older child or an adult at first. Ask questions such as, 'Who bought the book?' or 'What was it that cost fifty pence?', as well as matching the cards in threes.

Page 12 can be printed on to card and cut into two pieces, to help the children make up their own sets of three cards to add to the ready-printed ones.

Page 13 can be used by an individual child or by friends working together, and is especially effective if it is used as a way of recording role-play or real experiences.

Children enjoy setting up a pretend jumble sale, using toys and other items from around the classroom. Even better, taking part in a real sale helps their understanding of pricing, exchanging money for goods, and giving change.

The worksheet on page 32 also has a jumble sale theme.

Pages 14 and 15: The ten pence game

This game practises recognising coins and counting amounts of money up to ten pence. Print both pages on to card, and cover them with clear sticky plastic, if you wish, before cutting them up. Store the game in an A4 wallet.

Pages 16 and 17: The fifty pence game

This is a more difficult version of 'The ten pence game' on pages 14 and 15. Print both pages on to card, cover them with clear sticky plastic, if you wish, and cut them up. Store the instructions and the cards in an A4 wallet.

If you would like the children to play this game in groups of four or more, they will need more cards; print two copies of page 17, not just one.

Pages 18-23: Count-ups

These pages concentrate on counting up amounts of money using a mixture of coins.

Pages 18 and 19 can be cut up to make a flip-book of money puzzles. Print these pages on to paper; coloured paper is best, as the print may show through to the other side too much if you use white paper. Cut each page into three strips, along the horizontal dotted lines. Collect the sheets together in order, so that the strip from the top of page 18 is the front cover, and the strip from the bottom of page 19 is the back. Staple the book together with three or four staples along the top, just above the solid line.

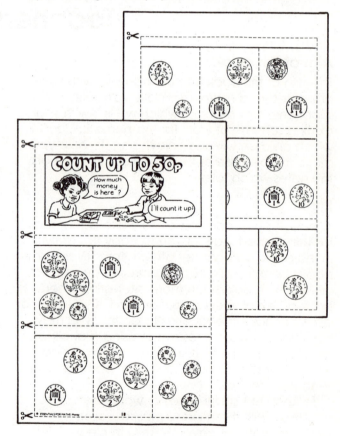

◆ ESSENTIALS FOR MATHS: Money

Finally, cut along the vertical dotted lines on the *four middle* pages, to make lift-up flaps.

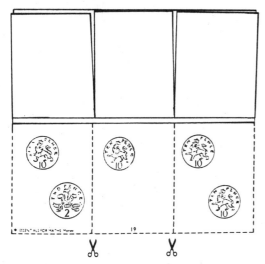

Pages 20 and 21 can be assembled in the same way to make a book of larger combinations, up to £1.

There are five pages showing three different groups of coins in each book, which means there are 5×5×5 possible combinations – 125 altogether in each book.

Children enjoy using these books, working in pairs to set questions for each other. Let them use coins or a calculator to check their work.

The worksheet on page 22 also requires the children to count up amounts of money using a variety of coins. When they have done this sheet, the children can each use one or more copies of page 23 to make up questions for each other. Coins can be drawn freehand, or you could provide rubber stamps (available from educational suppliers).

Pages 24 and 25: £5 notes and £10 notes

Print page 24 on to pale blue paper, and page 25 on to buff-coloured paper, to help distinguish between them. Before letting the children colour them in and cut them out, spend some time talking about real bank notes, and if possible show some real notes. Talk about why it is necessary for a bank note's design to be quite complicated (to avoid forgery) and point out that notes are printed on special paper, using several colours of printing ink, and with metal strips threaded through each note. Each note says how much it is worth in figures and in words, and £5 notes are slightly smaller than £10 notes.

Depending on the age and experience of the children, you may want to help them write successive serial numbers on each of their notes. There is space for a further two figures, so you could number the first £5 note R400 (in two places), the next one R401, and so on. Talk about the fact that if someone's money is damaged (for example, by being burned, or half-eaten by the dog!) the bank will replace it if pieces of the notes showing the serial numbers remain.

Pages 26 and 27: Teddy shops A and B

Print these pages on to card, or print them on to paper and mount them on card. Colour in the teddies, cover the cards with clear sticky plastic if you wish and cut them out. With younger or less-experienced children, you may want to use two copies of sheet A at first, rather than A and B.

Many children enjoy playing with these cards, on their own or in pairs, using plastic or card '£1 coins' (or counters or buttons to represent pound coins) and the £5 and £10 notes printed on pages 24 and 25.

Three or four children can play this game. They need a dice and some 'money'.
- One child is the shopkeeper and banker (or an adult or older child may take this role). She or he places the teddy cards in the centre of the table (perhaps on a sheet of coloured paper, as the shop), and gives each player a £5 note, a £10 note and five £1 coins.
- Each player in turn throws the dice, and the banker gives them that many pounds. The player can then buy a teddy from the shop, if he or she has enough money.
- The game continues until all the teddies are sold. Many children are happy to just say, 'The teddy shop's shut!' and compare what they have bought. Alternatively, each child could count up the total value of the teddies they have purchased, to decide on a winner.

Pages 28–30: Flap puzzles

Print these sheets on to paper, and cut them each into two pieces. Each flap puzzle is a reusable question, with the answer hidden under the fold-up flap. Flap puzzles 1 and 2 are simple ones; puzzles 3 and 4 are more difficult. Keep a collection of puzzles together for the children to use with partners (with coins, if you wish). Add to the collection using page 30, by writing puzzles of your own or getting the children to write them. Draw coins freehand, or use rubber stamps.

Page 31: Bus fares

When they have done this worksheet, you may want the children to go on making up problems for each other which involve giving change. For example, 'I gave the driver fifty pence. The fare was twenty-seven pence. How much change should I get?' Provide coins and a calculator to help.

Page 32: Jumble toys

You may want to link this worksheet to the activities described on pages 10 to 13.

National Curriculum: Mathematics

The activities in this book support the following requirements of the PoS for KS1 for the National Curriculum for mathematics:

Using and applying mathematics

Pupils should be given opportunities to:
- use and apply mathematics in practical tasks, in real-life problems and within mathematics itself;

Pupils should be taught to:
- select and use the appropriate mathematics;
- select and use mathematical equipment and materials.

Number

Pupils should be given opportunities to:
- develop flexible methods of working with number, orally and mentally;
- use a variety of practical resources and contexts;
- use calculators both as a means to explore number and as a tool for calculating with realistic data.

Pupils should be taught to:
- count orally up to 10 and beyond, knowing the number names; count collections of objects, checking the total;
- develop a variety of methods for adding and subtracting;
- explore and record patterns in addition and subtraction;
- recognise and use simple fractions, including halves and quarters, decimal notation in recording money;
- choose a suitable method of computation, using apparatus where appropriate, or a calculator where the numbers include several digits;
- sort and classify a set of objects using criteria related to their properties.

Scottish 5-14 Curriculum: Mathematics

In addition to the content of the attainment outcome 'Problem solving and enquiry', the following attainment outcomes and targets are relevant to the activities in this book:

Attainment outcome	Strand	Attainment targets	Level
Number, money and measurement	Money	Use 1p, 2p, 5p, 10p, 20p coins to buy things.	A
		Use coins up to £1 including exchange (50p = 5 x 10p).	B
		Use coins/notes to £5 worth or more, including exchange.	C
	Add and subtract	Add and subtract: in applications in money, including payments and change to 10p.	A
		Add and subtract: in applications in money, including payments and change up to £1.	B

See inside back cover for Northern Ireland Curriculum links

Games with coin cards

◆ Use the suggestions printed below, with the cards printed on pages 6 to 9, to provide practice at coin recognition and comparison.

◆ **Quick match-ups**
Shuffle the cards. How quickly can you sort the cards into groups of four, so that all the cards worth the same amount are together?

◆ **Pairs**
This is a game for 2 or 3 players.
Shuffle the cards and spread them out, face down. When it is your turn, turn over two cards. If they match, you can keep them. If they don't match, turn them back. Who can collect the most cards?

◆ **Who has most?**
This is a game for 2 players.
Shuffle the cards and spread them out, face down. Each of you must choose a card to turn over, at the same time. The person whose card shows the most money, keeps both cards. If they are the same amount, you keep one each. Who can collect the most cards?

Coin cards

Further cards are printed on pages 8 and 9.

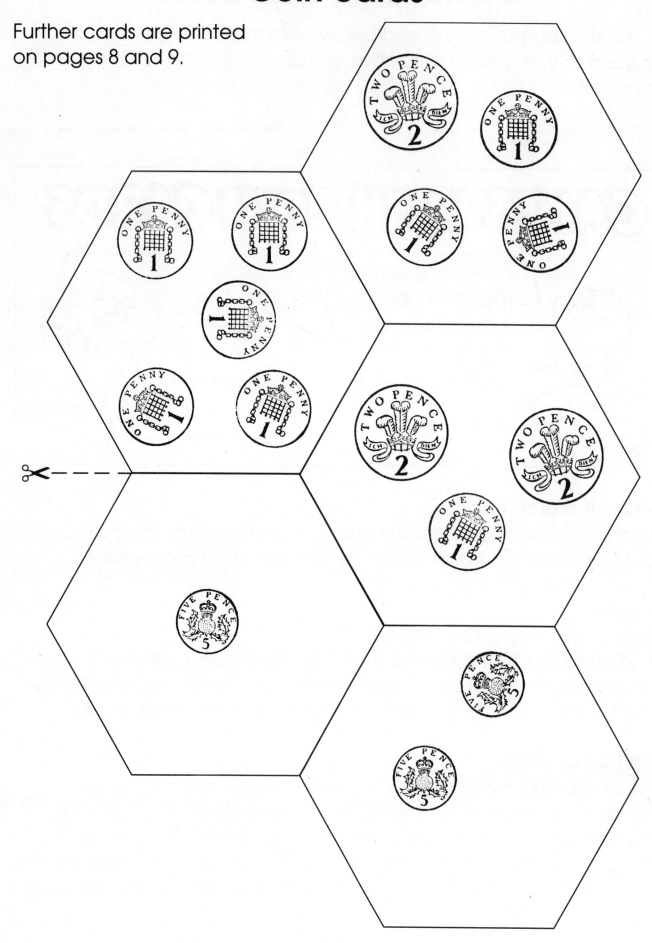

◆ ESSENTIALS FOR MATHS: Money

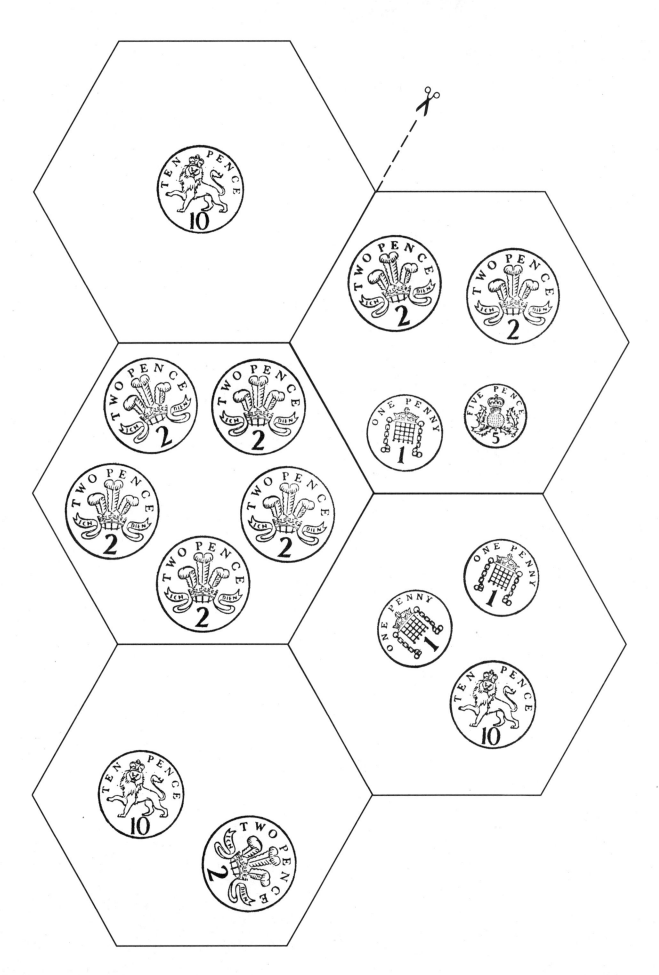

ESSENTIALS FOR MATHS: Money

More coin cards

To be used with those on pages 6 and 7.

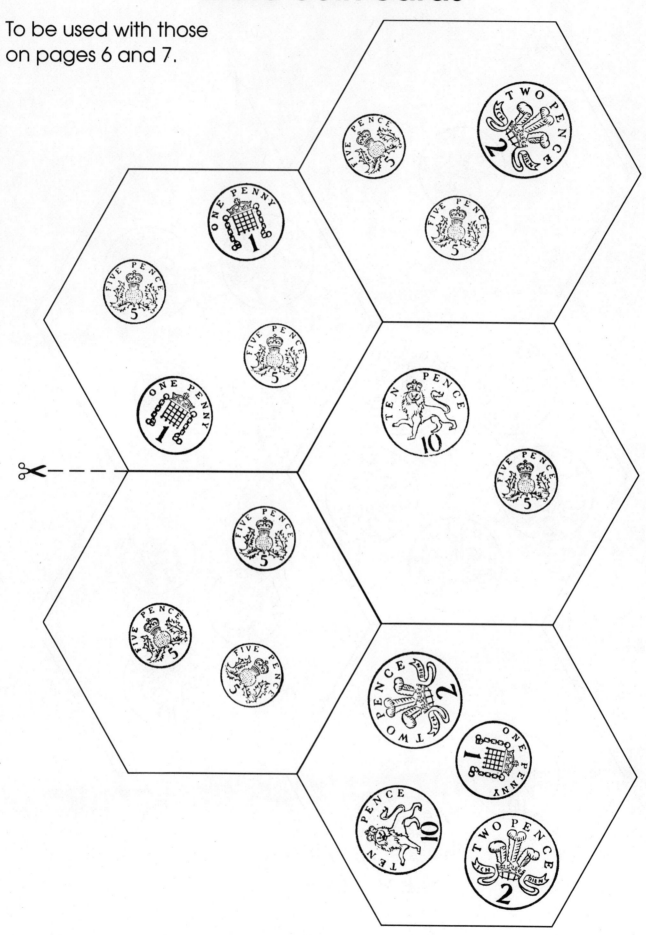

◆ ESSENTIALS FOR MATHS: Money

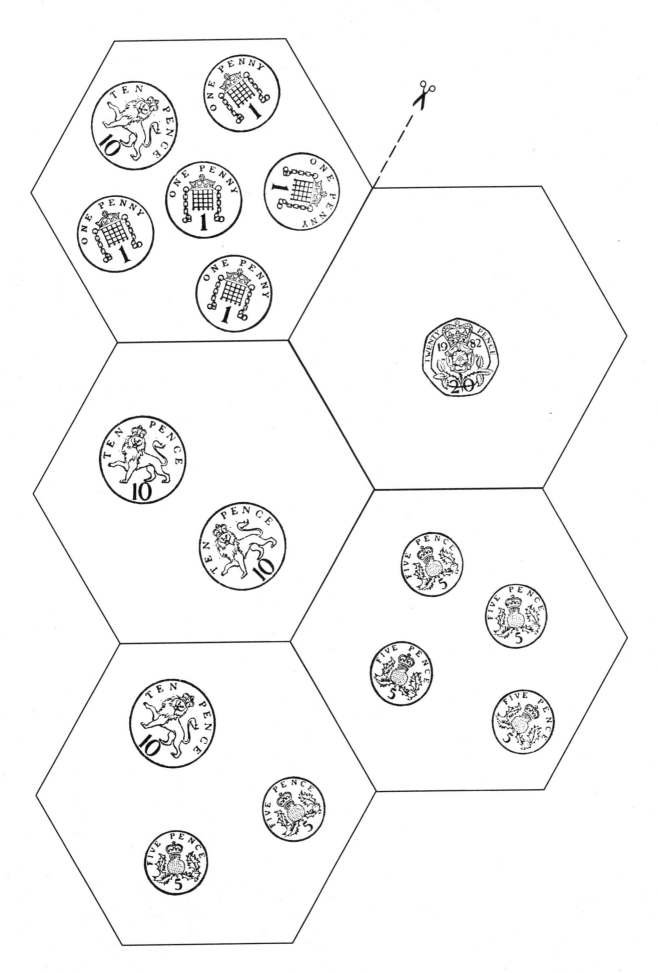

ESSENTIALS FOR MATHS: Money   9

Jumble Sale matching cards

◆ Can you match the people to the things they bought and the money they spent?

◆ ESSENTIALS FOR MATHS: Money

Make your own Jumble Sale matching cards

Make your own Jumble Sale matching cards

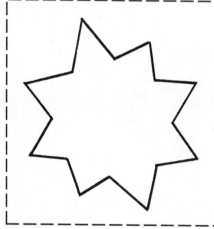

ESSENTIALS FOR MATHS: Money

Name _____

Jumble story

"I went to a jumble sale."

"Here's what I bought."

It cost

Here's how I paid:

ESSENTIALS FOR MATHS: Money

The ten pence game

◆ Use the instructions printed below, with the playing cards printed on page 15, to make this game.

A more difficult, but similar, game is on pages 16 and 17.

1 Shuffle the cards.
Put them in a pile, face down, in the middle.

2 Take it in turns to take a card from the top of the pile.
Put it face up, in front of you.

3 Add up how much money you've got as you go along.

4 If you reach exactly 10p, call out, 'TEN PENCE!'
You have won!

If you get <u>more</u> than 10p, call out 'BUST' and drop out of the game.

'The ten pence game' playing cards

The fifty pence game

◆ Use the rules printed below, with the playing cards printed on page 17, to make this game.

An easier version of the game is on pages 14 and 15.

1 Shuffle the cards.
Put them in a pile, face down, in the middle.

2 Take it in turns to take a card from the top of the pile.
Put your cards face up, in front of you.

3 Add up how much money you've got as you go along.

4 If you reach exactly 50p, call out, 'FIFTY PENCE!'
You have won!

If you get <u>more</u> than 50p, call out 'BUST' and drop out of the game.

'The fifty pence game' playing cards

ESSENTIALS FOR MATHS: Money

◆ ESSENTIALS FOR MATHS: Money

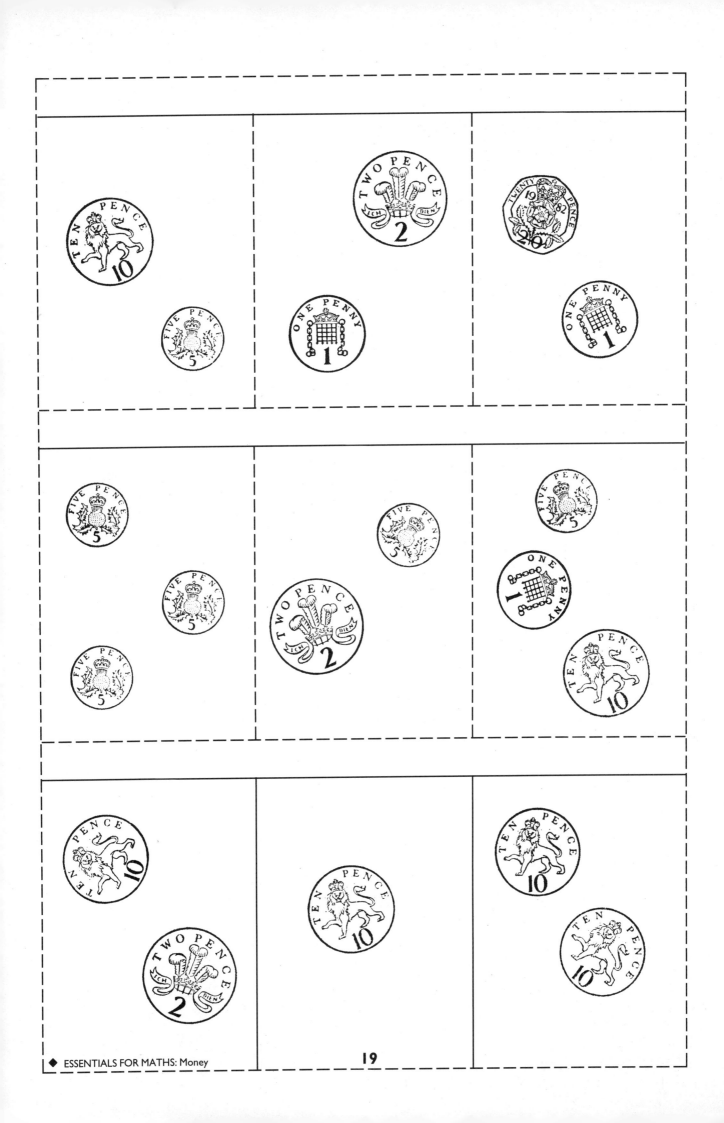

ESSENTIALS FOR MATHS: Money

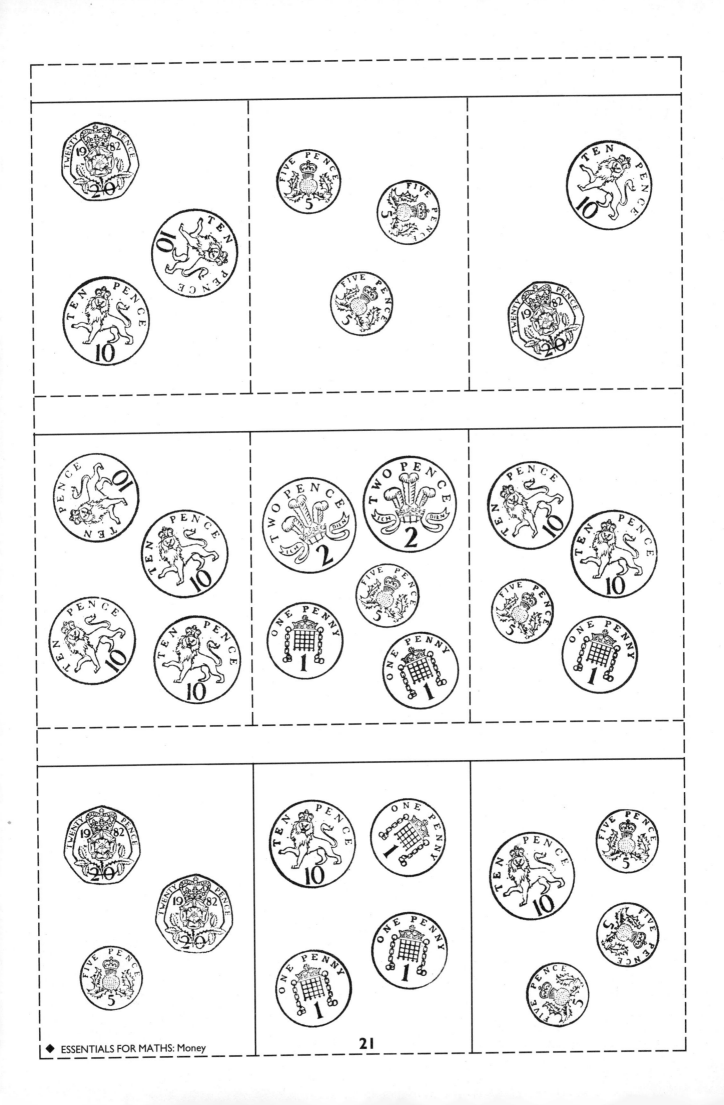

ESSENTIALS FOR MATHS: Money

21

◆ Name _____

Count-ups

How much money is in each box ?

Count it up !
Write your answers in the stars.

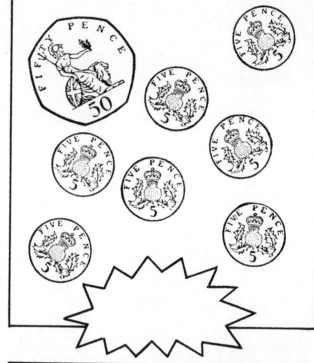

◆ ESSENTIALS FOR MATHS: Money

◆ Names _____ _____

More count-ups

Make up some questions for a friend to try.

Then check your friend's answers.

◆ ESSENTIALS FOR MATHS: Money

◆ Name _____

£5 notes

◆ Colour in these £5 notes. Each one should be the same.
◆ Write in the serial numbers. Should they be the same?
◆ Cut out the notes.

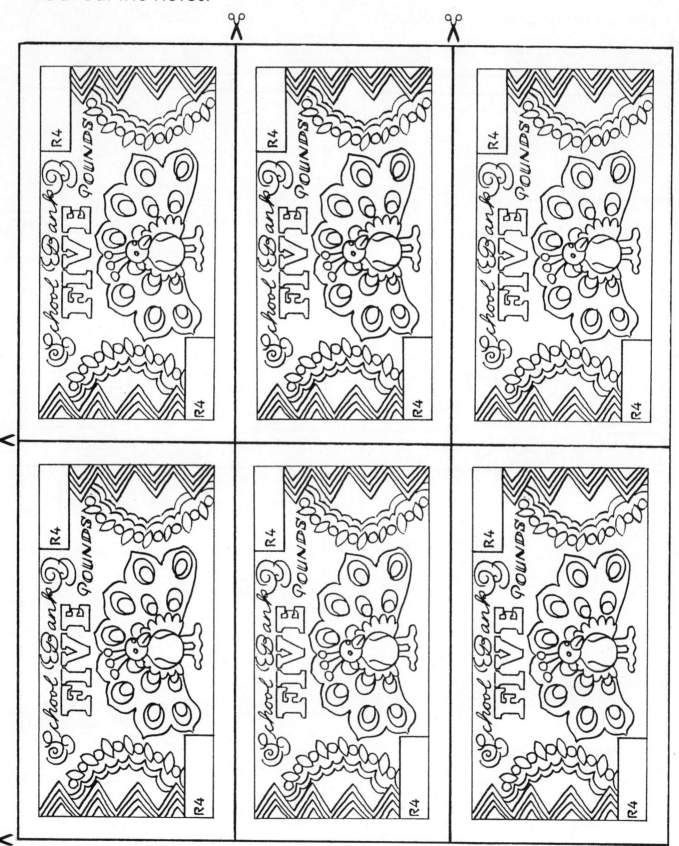

◆ ESSENTIALS FOR MATHS: Money

£10 notes

- Colour in these £10 notes. Each one should be the same.
- Write in the serial numbers. Should they be the same?
- Cut out the notes.

Teddy shop A

Teddy shop B

Flap puzzle 1

FOLD ➤

Flap puzzle 2

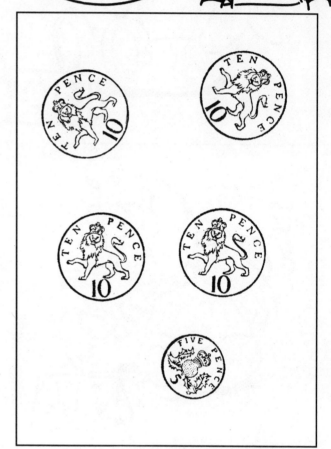

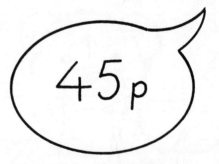

FOLD ➤

Flap puzzle 3

How much money have I got?

£7·50

FOLD ▶▶

Flap puzzle 4

How much money have I got?

£3·46

FOLD ▶▶

Flap puzzle ☐

"How much money have I got?"

FOLD »

This puzzle was made up by

_____

Flap puzzle ☐

"How much money have I got?"

FOLD »

This puzzle was made up by

_____

Bus fares

How could you give each bus driver exactly the right money?

27p please.

44p please.

36p please.

◆ Name _____

Jumble toys

I went to a jumble sale. Here's what I bought.

I paid with a 20p.

How much change did I get?

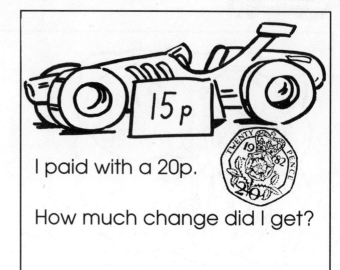

I paid with a 20p.

How much change did I get?

I paid with a 50p.

How much change did I get?

Use toys and coins to make up more puzzles like these for your friends.